W9-AOT-703

Energy at Work

Hydroelectric Power

by Josepha Sherman

Consultant:
Steve Brick, Associate Director
Energy Center of Wisconsin
Madison, Wisconsin

Capstone press®
Mankato, Minnesota

Fact Finders is published by Capstone Press
151 Good Counsel Drive, P.O. Box 669, Mankato, Minnesota 56002
www.capstonepress.com

Library of Congress Cataloging-in-Publication Data
Sherman, Josepha.
    Hydroelectric power / by Josepha Sherman.
    p. cm.—(Fact finders. Energy at work)
    Summary: Introduces the history, uses, production, advantages and disadvantages,
and future of hydroelectric energy as a power resource.
    Includes bibliographical references and index.
    ISBN-13: 978-0-7368-2472-9 (hardcover)   ISBN-10: 0-7368-2472-3 (hardcover)
    ISBN-13: 978-0-7368-5192-3 (softcover pbk.) ISBN-10: 0-7368-5192-5 (softcover pbk.)
    1. Hydroelectric power plants—Juvenile literature. [1. Hydroelectric power plants.
2. Water power.] I. Title. II. Series.
TK1081.S513 2004
333.91′4—dc22   2003015051

Editorial Credits
Gillia Olson, editor; Juliette Peters, designer; Alta Schaffer, photo researcher; Eric Kudalis,
    product planning editor

Photo Credits
Cover: Scrivener Dam on the Molongol River in Canberra, Australia, Index Stock
    Imagery/photolibrary.compty.ltd

Bureau of Reclamation, 16; Corbis/Royalty Free, 1, 6–7; Corbis/Yann Arthus-Bertrand, 19;
Energy Systems & Design Ltd., 25; Folio, Inc./Richard T. Nowitz, 5; Getty Images/David
McNew/Newsmakers, 22; Houserstock/Ellen Barone, 20–21; Hulton/Archive by Getty
Images, 10, 11; John Elk III, 12, 17; Jon Gnass/Gnass Photo Images, 23; North Wind Picture
Archives, 9; NREL/Duane Hippe, 27; Richard Cummins, 14–15; Thomas Kitchin/Tom
Stack & Associates, 13; TVA, 18; Wavegen, 26

2 3 4 5 6 09 08 07 06 05

Table of Contents

Chapter 1 Thundering Water 4

Chapter 2 Hydroelectricity. 6

Chapter 3 Water Power in History 8

Chapter 4 Generating Hydroelectricity. 14

Chapter 5 Benefits and Drawbacks 20

Chapter 6 The Future 24

Fast Facts 28

Hands On: Build a Dam 29

Glossary 30

Internet Sites. 31

Read More 31

Index 32

Thundering Water

The Niagara River creates the thundering Niagara Falls. This powerful river is also an energy source. Upstream of the falls, some of the river water flows into giant pipes. The water goes to power plants downstream. The plants use the water to make electricity for 1 million homes.

Canada and the United States limit the amount of river water used to make energy. During the busy summer, power plants can only use the water at night. They make sure visitors can always watch the thundering falls.

Niagara Falls lies on the border between New York in the United States and Ontario in Canada.

Chapter 2

Hydroelectricity

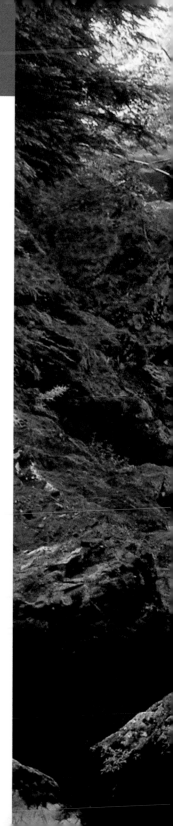

The Greek word *hydro* means water. Hydroelectricity is electricity made from moving water. People use rivers, ocean tides, and ocean waves to make hydroelectricity.

The water cycle makes hydropower a never-ending source of energy. Water **evaporates** from oceans, lakes, and rivers into a gas. The gas condenses into clouds. Later, it falls as rain and snow. Rain and snow refill rivers and lakes.

Hydroelectricity is a **renewable energy** source. Water is not used up to make hydroelectricity. Hydropower is the most common renewable energy source in the United States.

The Water Cycle

condensation

evaporation

precipitation

ocean

river

Hydroelectricity comes from the power of moving water.

Inset: The water cycle makes hydropower renewable.

Chapter 3

Water Power in History

People have used water power for thousands of years. Water power made work easier.

Water Mills

More than 2,000 years ago, Greeks used water mills to grind grain into flour. They built the mills next to rivers. The mill had a large wheel with blades that sat partly in the river. As the river flowed, the wheel turned. The wheel turned gears. The gears moved stones that ground the grain into flour. Water mills became popular around the world.

For thousands of years, people used water mills to grind grain into flour.

By the 1800s, people began using hydropower to run other machines. Water power turned spinning wheels to make thread. It ran weaving looms to make cloth. People also used water power to run sawmills.

Electricity

In 1879, Thomas Edison invented a long-lasting light bulb. The bulb needed electricity to work. Some people wanted to use water power to create electricity.

In 1880, the first plant to make hydroelectricity powered lights in the Wolverine Chair Factory. By 1889, 200 U.S. power plants were making hydroelectricity.

In the 1930s, the United States started many large **dam** projects. Building began on the Hoover Dam in 1931. By 1940, almost 40 percent of U.S. electricity came from hydropower.

The Hoover Dam was one of the many large dams built in the 1930s.

▲ A man stands on the intake pipes for a dam built in Ireland in the 1940s.

Hydroelectricity became an important energy source around the world. Canada, Russia, Brazil, China, and many other countries began using hydroelectric power. China alone built more than 80,000 hydroelectric projects after 1949.

Modern Use

In the United States, hydroelectricity did not keep up with power demands. More energy was needed as people used more electric machines. Most of the new power came from coal or nuclear power plants. Today, only 7 percent of U.S. energy comes from hydroelectricity.

The Sakakawea Dam and power plant sits on the plains of ▼ North Dakota.

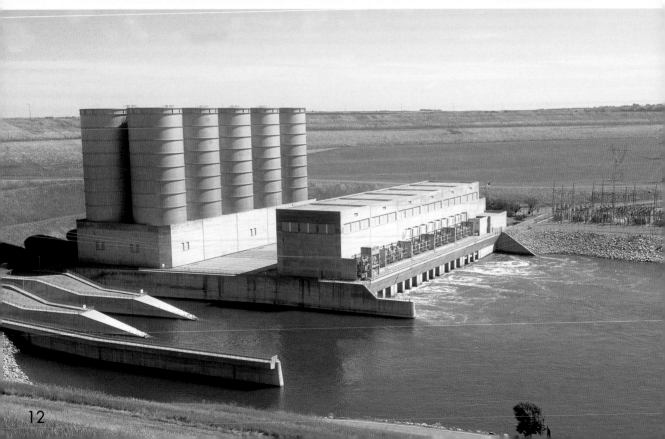

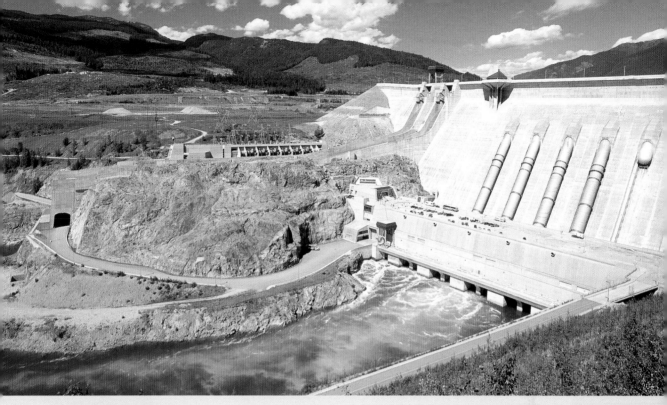

▲ Canada's dams, including this one in British Columbia, provide two-thirds of the country's power.

FACT!

Washington and Oregon get more than 85 percent of their electricity from hydropower.

Around the world, hydropower remains an important energy source. Two-thirds of Canada's electricity comes from hydropower. About 20 percent of the world's power comes from hydroelectricity.

Chapter 4

Generating Hydroelectricity

Most hydroelectric plants use dams built across rivers. Water enters huge pipes called **penstocks** that run through the dam. The water passes through **turbines** in the penstocks. Turbines look like huge fans. The turbines power generators. The **generator** makes electricity.

The amount of hydroelectricity created depends on two things. They are the height of the falling water and the amount of water. Large amounts of water falling from great heights create more energy.

Colorfully painted generators make electricity at the Raccoon Mountain pumped-storage plant in Tennessee.

▲ Workers replace one of the turbines in the Grand Coulee Dam.

Reservoirs

Some hydroelectric dams stop water from flowing downriver. Lakes called **reservoirs** form upstream of these dams. Power companies control the water flow through the penstocks in the dams.

Run-of-the-river systems do not create reservoirs. The natural water flow determines how much energy is made.

Top: Many dams hold water in a reservoir. The water flow through the dam is controlled.

Bottom: The Shasta Dam in California creates Lake Shasta.

➤

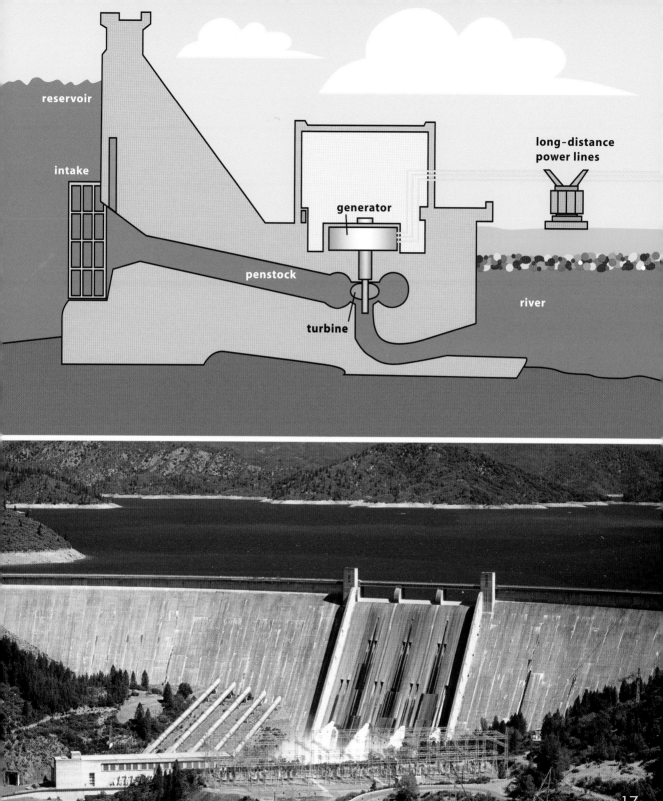

reservoir

intake

long-distance
power lines

generator

penstock

turbine

river

17

Pumped-Storage Plants

Pumped-storage plants are another type of hydroelectric plant. These plants have a reservoir built on a mountaintop or another high place. During the night, water is pumped uphill through a penstock to fill the reservoir. During the daytime, the water flows back down through the penstock, turning a turbine.

Tennessee's Raccoon Mountain pumped-storage plant takes water from the Tennessee River and stores it in a reservoir on
▼ Raccoon Mountain.

Pumped-storage plants use electricity to pump the water to the reservoir. But they use the power when outside demand is low. Costs to the plant are low.

Tidal Power

A few hydroelectric plants use tides to create electricity. People build a dam across an ocean inlet. As the tide comes in, the dam traps the rising water. As the tide goes out, the water is released. It flows over turbines to make electricity. Canada, France, Russia, and China have tidal power plants.

The tidal power station in La Rance, France, is the largest in the world. ➤

Chapter 5

Benefits and Drawbacks

Hydroelectric power is widely used around the world. But this power source is increasingly called into question. Like all power sources, it has benefits and drawbacks.

Benefits

Hydroelectricity is a renewable, clean energy source. Hydroelectric power plants do not produce **pollution**. Nonrenewable resources, such as coal and oil, pollute the air when burned to make energy.

The Glen Canyon Dam in Arizona created Lake Powell.

Reservoirs have many uses. They often provide farmers with water for crops. They also provide boating and other fun activities for visitors.

Drawbacks

Hydroelectric power plants that rely on rainfall can be undependable. **Droughts** reduce river water, leaving less water to make electricity.

Dams can harm the environment. When dams are built, areas upstream are flooded. Farmland and animal habitats are destroyed. A reservoir changes a river. It becomes more like a lake.

▲ In 2001, a drought reduced the water level of the reservoir behind the Grand Coulee Dam in Washington. Docks were stranded and electricity production slowed.

As water flows through dams, the water temperature changes. The change may kill fish and water plants.

Dams may harm fish in other ways. Fish that are sucked through turbines can die. Some dams stop salmon migration. Salmon swim upstream to lay their eggs. Dams block the salmons' passage, stopping them from reproducing.

People have built fish ladders to help salmon swim past dams. Salmon are good jumpers. The fish leap up a series of steps to get around the dam.

This fish ladder on the Columbia River is one way engineers try to reduce the impact of dams on fish. ▼

Chapter 6

The Future

The best places for large hydropower projects have been used. Few large hydropower projects are being built today. Small projects may become more common.

Microsystems

Microsystems are becoming more popular. They create enough electricity for a home or small town. Microsystems are usually run-of-the-river projects. Microsystems have more possible uses than large hydroelectric plants. Large projects must be built on large fast-flowing rivers. Microsystems can be built on smaller rivers.

The tiny turbine in this microsystem is smaller than a person's hand.

Wave Power

Waves can be used to make electricity. Oscillating water columns (OWCs) use wave energy. The OWC sits partly above and partly below the ocean's surface. As waves flow through it, air in the OWC is forced through turbines. The turbines generate electricity. Small OWCs are used in some European countries. More research is needed to learn how to keep OWCs from being damaged in storms.

⬆ Some wave power devices sit on coastlines to use the power of the crashing waves.

Hydropower will continue to be an important power source. New technology will help determine hydropower's future. The value people place on renewable, clean energy sources will also help determine the future of water power.

This relatively small hydropower dam in Alaska makes power for a remote village.

Fast Facts

- *Hydro* means water. Hydroelectricity is electricity made using water.

- Hydroelectricity is a renewable resource. Water is not used up to make electricity.

- Most hydroelectric power plants use dams. Water either builds up behind the dam in a reservoir or flows naturally through a dam in a run-of-the-river system.

- The first hydroelectric power plant was built in 1880 in Michigan. It powered 16 lights at the Wolverine Chair Factory.

- About 20 percent of the world's energy comes from hydropower, but only about 7 percent of the United States' energy comes from hydropower.

- Rivers are the most common hydropower sources. People also use ocean tides and waves to make hydroelectricity.

Hands On: Build a Dam

Today, most dams are made of concrete. Early dams were made of dirt and rock. Create your own dam and see if it will hold. Do this activity outside, as water may spill.

What You Need
rectangular plastic container
sand or dirt
flat, stackable rocks or plastic pieces
pebbles or gravel
pitcher or small pail of water

What You Do
1. Fill the bottom half of the container with sand or dirt.
2. Use your finger to dig a "riverbed" in the sand down the length of the container.
3. Pick a spot along the "river" for your dam.
4. Use the flat, stackable rocks or plastic pieces to build your dam. Use the pebbles or gravel to plug up any holes.
5. Gently pour water down the riverbed toward your dam. If the dam does not hold, what might fix it?

Glossary

dam (DAM)—a barrier built to block a body of water

drought (DROUT)—a long spell of very dry weather

evaporate (e-VAP-uh-rate)—to change from a liquid into a gas

generator (JEN-uh-ray-tur)—a machine that makes electricity by turning a magnet inside a coil of wire

penstock (PEN-stok)—intake pipes for a dam

pollution (puh-LOO-shuhn)—harmful materials that dirty or damage air, water, and soil

renewable energy (ri-NOO-uh-buhl EN-er-jee)—power from sources that can never be used up, such as wind, water, and the Sun

reservoir (REZ-ur-vwar)—a holding area for large amounts of water

turbine (TUR-bine)—an engine powered by water, steam, or gas passing through the blades of a fan and making it turn

Internet Sites

FactHound offers a safe, fun way to find Internet sites related to this book. All of the sites on FactHound have been researched by our staff.

Here's how:

1. Visit *www.facthound.com*
2. Type in this special code **0736824723** for age-appropriate sites. Or enter a search word related to this book for a more general search.
3. Click on the **Fetch It** button.

FactHound will fetch the best sites for you!

Read More

Draper, Allison Stark. *Hydropower of the Future: New Ways of Turning Water into Energy.* The Library of Future Energy. New York: Rosen Publishing Group, 2003.

Graham, Ian. *Water Power.* Energy Forever? Austin, Texas: Raintree Steck-Vaughn, 1999.

Oxlade, Chris. *Dams.* Building Amazing Structures. Chicago: Heinemann Library, 2001.

Snedden, Robert. *Energy Alternatives.* Essential Energy. Chicago: Heinemann Library, 2002.

Index

benefits, 20–21

Canada, 4, 5, 11, 13, 19
China, 11, 19

dam, 10, 14, 16, 19, 22, 23, 27
    Glen Canyon Dam, 21
    Grand Coulee Dam, 16, 22
    Hoover Dam, 10
drawbacks, 22–23
droughts, 22

electricity, 4, 6, 10, 13, 14, 15, 19, 22, 24, 26, 27
environment, 20, 22–23

fish, 23
fish ladders, 23

generator, 14, 15

microsystem, 24, 25

Niagara Falls, 4, 5

penstock, 14, 16, 18
pollution, 20
pumped-storage plant, 15, 18–19

reservoir, 16, 18, 19, 21, 22
run-of-the-river system, 16, 24

tidal power, 19
turbine, 14, 16, 18, 19, 23, 25, 26, 27

water cycle, 6, 7
water mills, 8, 9
wave power, 26